Books by Dave

Truth be Told: A journey from ...
The Little Book of OCD

The Little Book Of OCD

<> <> <>

Dave Preston

Published by Dave Preston

© Copyright 2016 Dave Preston

All rights reserved. No part of this book may be reproduced, scanned or distributed in any printed or electronic form without permission. Please do not participate in or encourage piracy of copyrighted materials in violation of the author's rights. Purchase only authorized editions.

Health & Wellness – Psychology – Addictions & Recovery - OCD
Health & Wellness – Psychology – Obsessive Compulsive Disorder

Version 1.00

Available on Kindle and other devices

Designed by Dave Preston

To my many friends at the OCD-UK forum.
Thanks for the education.

www.ocdforums.org

Author's Note

Most books on OCD these days, with the exception of memoirs, are written by psychologists and psychiatrists. There's good reason for that. OCD is a significant mental disorder that needs to be diagnosed by a professional and, preferably, treated by a professional. That said, the people whose lives OCD has turned upside down have knowledge about the disorder too.

I was an OCD sufferer for 40 years. I suffered terribly from multiple different kinds of obsessions along quite a few different themes. I suffered in silence. I told no one about the terrible thoughts in my head. After a mental health crisis, I sought help. After four decades, I was diagnosed with OCD, put on medications and received the proper kind of treatment for my disorder.

Today I am well. I consider myself an ex-sufferer because I no longer suffer from the disorder. Along the way, I became very educated about Obsessive Compulsive Disorder. I started my own blog where I write about OCD (www.ocdlife.ca) And I spent a lot of time on OCD forums, answering questions from sufferers, offering advice and an empathetic ear. I've amassed more than 10,000 posts on forums. I consider myself a layperson's authority on OCD.

Neither this book nor any other can replace the invaluable experience of working directly with a qualified mental health professional in developing and implementing a plan to effectively deal with OCD. I encourage everyone to seek professional help.

Dave Preston

What is OCD?

Obsessive Compulsive Disorder is a serious but treatable mental disorder that involves persistent, negative, intrusive thoughts or images (obsessions) and repetitive acts, behaviors or rituals (compulsions).

Previously the American Psychiatric Associated classified OCD as an anxiety disorder, alongside Generalized Anxiety Disorder, Panic Disorder and Social Anxiety Disorder. In the fifth edition of the Diagnostic and Statistical Manual of Mental Disorders (DSM-5), OCD is now a separate diagnosis with its own chapter, *Obsessive Compulsive and Related Disorders.*

The French once called OCD 'la folie de doute', which translates to 'the doubting disease'. They had it right. OCD involves obsessions and compulsions where doubt reigns supreme. Why does a man wash his hands 50 times a day? Because he doubts his hands are clean. Why does a woman check the stove is off for the tenth time in a row? Because she doubts the stove is off, no matter how many times she has checked.

The DSM, which is considered the gold standard diagnostic manual in North America, lists criteria for the diagnosis of OCD:

* Presence of obsessions, compulsions or both.

* The obsessions or compulsions are time consuming (Take more than one hour per day) or cause clinically significant distress or impairment in social, occupational or other important areas of functioning.

* The symptoms are not attributable to the physiological effects of a substance (drug abuse, a medication) or another medical condition.

* The disturbance is not better explained by the symptoms of another mental disorder (Such as Generalized Anxiety Disorder).

Pretty much everyone on the planet gets intrusive thoughts. From time to time bizarre or out of place thoughts pop up in our brains. Most people are able to dismiss these thoughts as irrelevant but it's a different story for OCD sufferers.

When OCD is involved, intrusive thoughts are taken as serious, alarming and in dire need of attention. Anxiety levels rise. The sufferer feels high levels of distress. In response, a compulsion is performed to try to alleviate the distress.

What is an obsession?

An obsession is an intrusive thought, image, impulse, urge or fear (or any combination of) that causes distress. That should be read as: *an obsession is an intrusive thought, intrusive image, intrusive impulse, intrusive urge or intrusive fear (or any combination of) that causes distress.*

But what does that mean? What's intrusive? Intrusive means causing disruption through being unwelcome and uninvited. So obsessions disrupt the sufferer because the thoughts, images, impulses, urges or fears they experience are unwelcome and uninvited. OCD sufferers don't ask for obsessions and when they get them, they really don't want them.

Some people think of intrusive thoughts as being somehow different from an obsession but they are not. Intrusive thoughts are simply a type of obsession. They are also the most common type of obsession.

Another way to think of obsessions is that they are thoughts, images, impulses, urges or fears that just pop into the sufferer's head. Sufferers don't do anything to make the thoughts, etc. pop up. The obsessions just show up on their own accord, without invitation or the sufferer doing anything to make them appear.

An important thing to know about obsessions is that they are both intrusive and cause distress. It is possible to get an intrusive thought without it causing distress and, in that case, it would not be an OCD obsession.

What kind of distress do OCD sufferers experience? The majority of sufferers describe the distress they experience as anxiety. In fact, OCD is a type of anxiety disorder and the majority of sufferers do experience heightened levels of anxiety, especially immediately following an obsession. Other types of distress experienced include guilt, shame, fear and disgust.

Obsessions themselves tend not to last a long time (in fact they can be very short in duration), but they also tend to be repetitive. This is another distinction that is important – having one or two intrusive thoughts that cause distress would not qualify for a diagnosis of OCD but things become a problem when a sufferer experiences obsessions (either the same obsession, variations on a theme or over multiple themes) repeatedly.

Obsessions are not directly controllable. There has been no mechanism found that will give a sufferer the ability to directly control or stop obsessions. What can be controlled is how sufferers respond to obsessions.

Types of obsessions

There are as many types of obsessions as there are things out there that could possible freak someone out. If it could possibly cause distress (anxiety, guilt, shame, fear, disgust, etc.) then it could be an obsession.

Every website on OCD and OCD book has a list of the more common types of obsessions. Sometimes this causes a problem for some sufferers because they can't find their very specific obsession on any list. That doesn't mean they aren't experiencing obsessions. It simply points to lists that are not as exhaustive as the brain's ability to conjure up disturbing thoughts or images.

If you can't find your specific obsession on a list, don't worry. Go back to the basics: Is what you are experiencing a thought, image, urge, impulse, fear (or combination thereof)? Is it intrusive (unwanted/uninvited)? Do they just pop up in your head? Do they cause you distress? Do they lead you to perform some kind of compulsion? If so, you're probably dealing with an obsession.

Obsessions are loosely categorized in themes, with each theme containing many types of obsessions. Following is a list of common obsession themes and types. It is a modified version of the obsession list found on the YBOCS (Yale Brown Obsessive Compulsive Scale).

Aggressive obsessions
- Fear the sufferer might harm him/herself.
- Fear the sufferer might harm others.
- Violent or horrific images (such as murder, dismembered bodies).
- Fear of blurting out obscenities or insults.

- Fear the sufferer will act on unwanted impulses.
- Fear of doing something embarrassing.
- Fear the sufferer will steal things.
- Fear the sufferer will harm others because they are not careful enough.
- Fear the sufferer will be responsible for something terrible happening.

Contamination obsessions
- Concerns or disgust with bodily waste or secretions.
- Fears of contracting AIDS or other diseases from touching people/objects.
- Concern with dirt or germs.
- Excessive concern with environmental contaminants (asbestos, radiation, etc.)
- Excessive concern with household items (kitchen cleansers, solvents, etc.)
- Excessive concern with animals or animal waste.
- Bothered by sticky substances or residues.
- Concern that the sufferer will get ill because of a contaminant.
- Concern that the sufferer will get others ill because of spreading a contaminant.
- Fear that certain objects, words, numbers, phrases have become contaminated.

Sexual obsessions
- Sufferer has forbidden or perverse sexual thoughts, images, impulses.
- Unwanted thoughts/images about sexually abusing children.

- Worries/fears that the sufferer could be homosexual when they identify as heterosexual.
- Worries/fears that the sufferer could be heterosexual when they identify as homosexual.
- Aggressive sexual thoughts toward others (adult strangers, friends, family members).

Hoarding/Saving obsessions
- Worries about throwing out seemingly unimportant things that might be needed in the future.
- Urges to pick up/collect useless things.

Religious obsessions
- Scrupulosity: Concern with sacrilege, blasphemy.
- Excessive concern with right/wrong, morality.

Symmetry and exactness
- Accompanied by magical thinking (things must be 'right' or something bad will happen.
- Not accompanied by magical thinking.

Miscellaneous obsessions
- Need to know or remember certain things.
- Fear of saying certain things.
- Fear of not saying just the right thing.
- Fear of losing things.
- Intrusive (non-violent) images.
- Intrusive nonsense sounds, words or music (ex: A song in the mind that can't be stopped).
- Bothered by certain sounds/noises.
- Lucky/unlucky numbers.

- Colors with special significance.
- Superstitious fears (Fear of passing a black cat or cemetery).
- Guilt over doing something horrendous in the past, despite assurances that the incident was minor in nature.
- False memory: Experiencing intrusive thoughts that the sufferer did something very bad in the past despite there being no proof the incident occurred.

Somatic obsessions
- Concerns with illness or disease (Worried about having AIDS, cancer, despite reassurances from doctor).
- Excessive concern with body part or aspect of appearance.

What is a compulsion?

A compulsion is an action, behavior, ritual or mental ritual meant to alleviate the distress caused by obsessions.

It is important to note the second part of the definition: meant to alleviate the distress caused by obsessions. There's a reason why sufferers perform compulsions and that is to try and get rid of or negate the distress they feel when they get obsessions.

Sufferers think they have to perform compulsions in order to get relief from obsessions. Because obsessions tend to be repetitive, so are compulsions. Sufferers end up doing the same compulsion repeatedly.

Compulsions don't work; at least not in the long term. They can bring temporary relief but soon enough the obsession causing the problem crops up again, requiring another compulsion to be performed. It can become an endless cycle of obsessions and compulsions.

Actions or behaviors are specific things done by the sufferer to offset an obsession. An example of that would be washing hands after getting an obsession about contamination of the hands. A ritual would be like spending an hour before leaving the house, checking every electric appliance to make sure they are off in a systematic way. Mental rituals include having to say a positive word to negate a negative word.

Perhaps the most common compulsion among OCD sufferers is ruminating. To ruminate means to think deeply about something. In psychology, it means the compulsively focused attention on the symptoms of one's distress, and on its possible causes and consequences. It means to go over and over an intrusive thought and what it means without coming to a conclusion or answer.

There's something else about compulsions that everyone should know. Not only do they not work but also they backfire. Sufferers think they have to perform compulsions to alleviate the distress brought on by obsessions. However, what compulsions actually do is draw attention to the obsessions, highlighting their importance and guaranteeing the obsessions will come back, strong, in the future.

Types of compulsions

There are many different types of compulsions. The list below is by no means exhaustive but it gives an overview of the more common types of compulsions that exist. It has been modified by the list of compulsions found in the YBOCS.

Cleaning/washing compulsions
- Excessive or ritualized hand washing. (Washing hands many times a day or for an extended length of time after touching or thinking you have touched a contaminated object).
- Excessive or ritualized showering, bathing, tooth brushing, grooming or toilet routine.
- Excessive or ritualized cleaning of household items or other inanimate objects.
- Other measures meant to prevent or remove contact with contaminants.

Checking compulsions
- Checking locks, stove, appliances, electric plugs, etc.
- Checking that the sufferer did not/will not harm others.
- Checking that the sufferer did not/will not harm himself or herself.
- Checking that nothing terrible did/will happen.
- Checking that the sufferer did not make a mistake.
- Checking linked to somatic obsessions (Seeking reassurance from friends or doctors that the sufferer is not having a heart attack or getting cancer.

Repeatedly taking pulse, blood pressure or temperature. Checking for body odors. Checking appearance in a mirror).

Repeating compulsions
- Rereading or rewriting.
- Need to repeat routine activities.

Counting compulsions
- Need to count or recount.

Ordering/arranging compulsions
- Need to order and reorder, arrange and rearrange things.

Hoarding/collecting compulsions
- Compulsions to hoard or collect things.

Miscellaneous compulsions
- Mental rituals (Thinking a good thought to undo a bad thought).
- Ruminating (Going over an obsession in the sufferers head, repeatedly).
- Praying (Saying a prayer to undo an intrusive thought or image).
- Need to tell, ask or confess.
- Need to touch, tap or rub.
- Avoidance (Avoiding knives out of fear the sufferer will stab someone).
- Ritualized eating behaviors.

- Superstitious behaviors (Not taking a bus or train if its number contains an unlucky number).
- Reassurance seeking (Need to seek reassurance from family, friends, others that you are not a bad person, that you won't stab someone with a knife or that you won't sexually abuse a child).

What about Pure O?

There is a lot of talk about Pure O on the web and in OCD books. The fact is, Pure O is a misnomer and doesn't really mean a whole lot.

Pure O means pure obsession or purely obsessional. It was thought, at one time, that there was a category of OCD sufferers who only experienced obsessions with no corresponding compulsions. Over time, this was proved false. All OCD sufferers perform some kind of compulsion.

Nowadays Pure O means a type of OCD where the compulsions are covert, rather than overt. A covert compulsion would be ruminating – it can't be 'seen' by others. An overt compulsion would be washing hands – it can be 'seen' by others. Therefore, in reality, Pure O doesn't mean only obsessions. It's still OCD, with obsessions and compulsions in play.

Pure O has also come to be known as an overarching theme of OCD of certain types of obsessions experienced by sufferers. According to some people, obsessions such as aggressive obsessions (involving harm/aggression towards self or others) and sexual obsessions belong in the Pure O category. At the end of the day, it doesn't mean much. Pure O, whatever you think it means, is still OCD like all types of OCD and is treated the same way as all other types of OCD.

What causes OCD?

We don't know. That's the simple answer.

Research has been done on the cause of OCD but there doesn't seem to be one cause evident; there is no smoking gun at this point.

There is some evidence that levels of the neurotransmitter serotonin in the brain have something to do with OCD. Indeed, many sufferers who take an SSRI (Selective Serotonin Reuptake Inhibitor) are helped to varying degrees. Then there are people who aren't. Still others are helped by taking an SSRI and an anti-psychotic (which regulates other neurotransmitters in the brain), but not everyone who takes that combination sees a significant reduction in OCD symptoms.

Brain scans have shown that certain regions of the brains of OCD sufferers are hyperactive. Whether this means there is a genetic predisposition to OCD or it is caused by a learned response remains unclear.

Some children exhibit signs of OCD after a severe infection such as strep. This is called Pediatric Autoimmune Neuropsychiatric Disorders Associated with Streptococcal infection (PANDAS).

The jury is still out on whether environment has anything to do with OCD and it is not yet clear how much a role genetics plays in the formation of the disorder.

Regardless the cause of the disorder, it is known what works to help people tame their OCD.

OCD severity

OCD comes in different levels of severity, based on the effects of obsessions and compulsions on daily living.

Severity in OCD does not refer to the type of obsessions a sufferer has. This is a misguided belief that has cropped up on the web where some people promote the idea that some types of obsessions are worse than others. In reality, any type of obsession can be just as bad as or worse than any other.

OCD ranges from mild to moderate, severe to extreme. Those with mild forms of OCD are affected minimally by the disorder and tend to lead productive lives. Those with extreme forms of the disorder suffer debilitating consequences. Some people end up confined to their homes or even one or two rooms for many years because of their OCD.

The severity of OCD can be rated by a sufferer, either on his/her own or with the assistance of a mental health professional. Google 'YBOCS' and click on one of the links. The YBOCS includes a rating scale to determine how mild or severe a case of OCD is present. It can be a valuable tool to the sufferer.

How common is OCD?

At one time OCD was considered to be a rare disorder, likely due to misdiagnoses by untrained healthcare professionals and due to reluctance by sufferers to talk about their symptoms.

Trying to figure out how many people out there have Obsessive Compulsive Disorder can be a daunting task. Many studies have been conducted and few come up with the same number.

Generally speaking, studies show that between one and three percent of the population will have OCD at some point in their lives. On average, two per cent of any population has OCD. That works out to 1 in every 50 people.

That translates into more than 140 million worldwide, more than six million in the United States, 1.3 million in Great Britain and 700,000 in Canada.

The reason that it is difficult to pin down a more precise number is that OCD tends to be under-reported. It can take 10 to 15 years or more from the onset of symptoms for sufferers to seek help. In addition, many sufferers feel afraid, embarrassed, even shameful about their symptoms, leading to them trying to keep their obsessions and compulsions a secret. This causes delays in receiving treatment.

What OCD is not

OCD used to be a very little known mental disorder. Over time awareness of the disorder has grown, but so too has the frequency of using OCD to mean something that has little or no connection to the disorder.

Using OCD or the words obsessive and compulsive together incorrectly leads to furthering the misunderstanding surrounding the disorder. It trivializes and belittles the real suffering that goes along with the disorder.

Common these days are references, in speech, in text messages, on the World Wide Web and in social media platforms to people being a little OCD, a little bit OCD or a bit OCD. The sayings are meant to convey temporary fits of cleaning or organizing that is wrongly connected to OCD. These fits have nothing in common with Obsessive Compulsive Disorder. They rarely cause distress or anxiety, which is a part of real OCD.

In addition, OCD is not:
- Associated with being obsessed with hockey, soccer, shopping or any other enjoyable pastime. OCD sufferers do not take enjoyment from their disorder.
- Linked to collecting, as in collecting memorabilia, stamps, coins or other items. Hoarding is a recognized subtype of OCD. Collectors like to show off their collections and talk about them, while hoarders are not proud of their collections, which are typified by the hoarding of basically useless items.

- Associated with an obsession, such as that exhibited by a crazed stalker. That's a completely different kind of obsession.
- Linked to being a compulsive shopper, gambler or liar. Those are likely to be addiction problems and are linked to Impulse Control Disorders. These types of people may experience anxiety later on but there was no intrusive obsession that sparked the compulsive behavior.

OCD can come and go

Like many mental disorders, OCD can wax and wane over time. Some days are good; some days are bad. There are several things that can cause OCD symptoms to worsen and that are often talked about on OCD forums on the web.

The first and most important cause for OCD to get bad is stress. There is no indication that stress causes OCD but it can certainly make OCD symptoms worse.

Stress, such as brought on by a bad day at work, a hectic night at home with kids, divorce, moving, a death in the family or any number or other stressors can cause the frequency and severity of obsessions to hit the roof, requiring more time and effort on compulsions.

When the stressor is eliminated or dissipates, it is often found that OCD symptoms subside… until the next stressor hits.

The other thing that can cause OCD to spike is the female menstrual cycle. OCD forums are rife with stories from women who complain that that time of the month has caused their OCD to worsen. Equally compelling are stories about how, once the menstrual cycle is over, OCD subsides in severity.

OCD treatment

With the exception of OCD brought on by PANDAS (which is treated typically with a regimen of antibiotics), the treatment found to be most effective in treating OCD, and considered to be the gold standard treatment for the disorder, is Cognitive Behavioral Therapy (CBT) with an emphasis on Exposure and Response Prevention (ERP), with or without medications.

OCD is chronic. That means it persists or keeps coming back. Left unchecked OCD will fester and worsen. It can become all consuming. That is why it is very important for the sufferer to start getting help the moment they've figured out they might be dealing with the disorder.

Just as people with diabetes can learn to manage their disease through diet and exercise, people with OCD can learn to manage their disorder so that it does not adversely affect their daily living and improve their quality of life.

No matter the severity of OCD present, improvement is possible. Some people have been able to recover completely from their disorder to the point where they consider themselves ex-sufferers.

The best way to get on the road to recovery is to see a mental health professional for a diagnosis and to access CBT/ERP. A discussion about medications will likely happen. The first step is to see your GP.

Some people choose to begin their recovery on their own, to varying degrees of success. The best outcomes are realized when a professional sets up a plan of action with the sufferer and the sufferer works hard to meet the goals in the plan.

It is important that a sufferer contemplating setting out on the road to recovery becomes educated about OCD (that's why you're reading this book!) and about their version of OCD, including the recommended treatment. Not all healthcare professionals can recognize the symptoms of OCD, including obsessions and compulsions, and may not know where to send the sufferer for help. In this case, the sufferer, with foreknowledge, can help guide the process along.

Although not a treatment for OCD, per se, many people find relaxation therapies and/or mindfulness to be helpful during the recovery process.

Medications

Whether to go on medications for OCD is a personal choice best left to the sufferer and his/her GP or psychiatrist. Knowledge is power and there are some things about medications everyone should know.

Different people respond differently to OCD medications. There is no hard and fast rule as to how medications will help, if at all, everyone who takes them.

Some people find common medications take the edge off anxiety, allowing them to concentrate on a treatment plan based on CBT/ERP. Some people do not respond at all to medications, even after trying a number of them. Still others find their symptoms (frequency and severity of obsessions, need to perform compulsions) diminished moderately to greatly while taking medications.

Medications come with side effects. Some people barely notice side effects while others have such severe reactions to a medication that they have to stop taking them. Others experience side effects that subside over time. Always be aware of the likely side effects you could experience if you are considering going on an OCD medication.

Only taking medications to recover from OCD is not recommended. The web is replete with stories of OCD sufferers who took medications, got better to some degree, and then went off the medications only to find they were right back to square one again. Medications do not cure OCD but they can help for some people.

The most commonly prescribed medication for OCD is anti-depressants, notably a class of anti-depressant called SSRIs (Selective Serotonin Reuptake Inhibitors). There are quite a number of them and they include:

Generic Name (Trade Name)
- Citalopram (Cipramil/Celexa)
- Escitalopram (Cipralex)
- Fluoxetine (Prozac)
- Fluvaxamine (Luvox/Faverin)
- Paroextine (Paxil/Seroxat)
- Sertraline (Lustral/Zoloft)

A less commonly prescribed medication for OCD is the non-selective Serotonin Reuptake Inhibitor clomipramine (Anafranil). There tends to be more side effects with this drug than SSRIs and it affects more neurotransmitters than just serotonin.

Some psychiatrists prescribe an anti-psychotic along with an SSRI in the treatment of OCD. Anti-psychotics include Rispiradone (risperdal) and Abilify (aripiprazole). Once again, these drugs come with possible side effects and knowledge is power.

Cognitive Behavioral Therapy

The gold standard treatment for OCD is CBT (Cognitive Behavioral Therapy) with ERP (Exposure and Response Prevention), with or without medications.

Studies suggest that 75 per cent of those sufferers who received CBT are significantly helped. There are no risks or side effects to this form of therapy when it comes to treating OCD.

CBT is a combination of two types of therapy: Cognitive therapy, which looks to change the way a sufferer thinks; and behavioral therapy, which looks to change the way a sufferer behaves. ERP is a special type of behavioral therapy.

The goal of CBT is not to learn how not to have intrusive thoughts/obsessions. In fact, that would be pointless, since everyone gets intrusive thoughts. They happen all the time. What CBT is for is to learn to react differently to the obsessions that will come up in the future.

CBT teaches the sufferer that the thoughts themselves are not the problem; it is what the sufferer does with the thoughts and how they react to them that is the problem.

From a cognitive perspective, a sufferer can begin to learn to think about intrusive thoughts differently. Those thoughts, which used to be taken as being extremely negative, can be looked at as irrelevant, meaningless mind junk that can be dismissed without worry.

Cognitively, it is better to take a non-committed attitude about obsessions than it is to do the usual and argue against what the obsession stands for. For example, if a sufferer gets an intrusive thought that they could stab their partner with a knife, the usual result might be to argue internally that that would never happen, that the sufferer would never harm another person. All that does is brings attention to the obsession, guaranteeing it will come back in the future. Instead, the sufferer should think, immediately after the obsession pops up, that maybe they will stab their partner tonight. Then leave the whole matter alone.

With cognitive therapy, sufferers can learn that intrusive thoughts are just thoughts and don't mean anything. They are simply brain noise that pops up from time to time and they can be safely ignored as irrelevant.

From a behavioral perspective, a sufferer can learn that they don't have to behave the way they normally do every time an obsession strikes. And how do they normally behave? They perform compulsions. In other words, CBT, particularly ERP, teaches the sufferer to stop doing compulsions.

Exposure and Response Prevention

ERP is widely hailed as a breakthrough therapy for the treatment of OCD. It goes hand in hand with cognitive therapy and the practice of eliminating compulsions. It is all about challenging OCD directly.

ERP is composed of two parts: the exposure, where the sufferer exposes himself/herself to the subject of intrusive thoughts, and response prevention, where the sufferer practices not doing compulsions.

A qualified therapist will usually help a sufferer develop a hierarchy of obsessions and compulsions. This is done by listing out all the obsessions and compulsions that need to be dealt with and then ranking them on the amount of anxiety/distress caused by each obsession or the anxiety/distress the sufferer feels would be caused by not performing each compulsion.

With a ranked hierarchy (from least anxiety provoking to most anxiety provoking) in hand, the sufferer can begin ERP on the items at the bottom of the list first, tackling the easier obsessions/compulsions to start with.

For each item on the list, the sufferer exposes himself/herself to the obsession and then practices not performing the usual compulsion associated with that compulsion. This is done repeatedly until, over time, the sufferer experiences less and less anxiety doing so. Eventually the sufferer barely notices anxiety/distress after an exposure. At that point, it's time to move up one step on the list to the next obsession/compulsion.

Take the case of a sufferer who can't stand to touch 'dirty' things. If he does, he washes his hands for 10 minutes at a time, sometimes with bleach. The sufferer would make a list of things he would try to avoid touching. Perhaps one is a garbage can. As part of ERP, the sufferer touches a garbage can (the exposure) and then sits and waits without washing his hands (response prevention). Repeated sessions of this should lessen his anxiety about touching garbage cans. Next, the sufferer could up the ante, so to speak, to rubbing his hand all over a garbage can and then rubbing his face with the same hand (exposure). Again, the sufferer would have to forego washing his hands or at least delaying it for a specified time (response prevention).

ERP is typically done at a specified time, after work each day, for instance. The more ERP is done, the faster it will work. Sufferers should know there is a limit to the amount of exposures they can do before they need a break. Typically, exposures are done perhaps once per day until the exposures no longer raise anxiety levels significantly. A well-motivated sufferer might decide to do exposures twice a day.

The idea with ERP is to cause anxiety levels to rise with the exposure, then sit and wait for anxiety levels to lower back down to near normal levels, without doing compulsions in the process. When anxiety has lowered, the ERP session is over. In time, the sufferer should notice that their anxiety peaks at a lower and lower level and their anxiety returns to a normal level in a shorter and shorter time-period. This is evidence that ERP is working.

Therapists will often give the sufferer a chart to work with when doing ERP. Columns are labeled for date, ERP start time, starting anxiety level, peak anxiety level, ERP end time and end anxiety level. Anxiety levels are rated on a scale of 1 to 10, 1 being completely relaxed and 10 being near panic attack. The sufferer records the necessary information on the chart and can see, over repeated exposures, whether they are improving.

Examples of ERP in action

Betty normally washes her hands three times, for 10 minutes each, after she uses the washroom. She sets a goal to wash her hands once, for 45 seconds at most, after using the washroom. Switching from one extreme to another suddenly would be too big a change so Betty decides on a staged change (like a hierarchy) to accomplish the goal. She begins by cutting back to two instances of hand washing of 10 minutes each after using the washroom. (She is exposed to the problem, using the washroom, and she is, slowly, preventing the normal response to the problem.) At first, her anxiety levels go quite high not doing the usual three hand washing routines, but after successive attempts, her anxiety levels stay moderate. Once that is accomplished, Betty cuts back to one, 10-minute hand washing after using the washroom. Eventually she is able to cut back the time spent washing to 7.5 minutes, then 5 minutes, then 3 minutes, then 1 minute and finally to 45 seconds. This takes months to accomplish but eventually Betty reaches her goal, one step at a time.

Randy suffers from unwanted thoughts of a sexual nature toward children. In response, he performs the compulsion of avoidance (staying away from children) and ruminating. Randy's obsessions are often triggered by seeing a child. Randy begins his ERP by looking at a picture of child, allowing the usual intrusive thoughts/images to surface and then practicing not ruminating over them. Instead, he just looks at the picture and lets the thoughts/images run their course. His anxiety level goes up and stays up for a while but gradually it begins to diminish. This is a lesson that those going through ERP soon learn: anxiety levels will, for the most part, return to lower levels all on their own without having to perform compulsions. Randy practices this scenario repeatedly until looking at a picture barely raises his anxiety. Eventually he switches to the real thing, by being near children. He goes to a shopping mall and allows himself to be close to children, allowing the intrusive thoughts/images to appear and practicing not reacting to them. He does this repeatedly until he no longer gets anxiety spikes seeing a child. As with Betty, it takes months for Randy to see the full benefit of ERP. Eventually he becomes okay with being around children and even though he still gets negative thoughts, he barely pays attention to them.

Relaxation and mindfulness

As noted before, stress makes OCD worse. It makes sense then, that reducing stress can make OCD better.

Relaxation and mindfulness do not cure OCD. They don't directly make obsessions, or the need to perform compulsions, go away. However, learning to relax and be in the moment can make for a relaxed, less stressed person and that can have benefits when it comes to dealing with OCD.

Resources to learn relaxation and mindfulness are nearly endless. Lessons abound on the web. YouTube has many videos that can guide you through exercises. There are many books on the subject. Check with your GP or local mental health organization to find out if there are relaxation groups in your area.

You are in charge

If you are an adult and you suffer from OCD, you are in charge of your recovery. If you are the parent of a child with OCD, you are in charge of your child's recovery.

Don't ever think that you need to sit back and let things happen. It's up to you to become knowledgeable about OCD, to communicate with your GP and mental health professional, to set expectations for recovery and to do the work necessary to see recovery become a reality.

If you are considering medications, you are in charge of asking questions about how they work and possible side effects.

If your GP sends you or your child to a therapist, you are in charge of making sure that therapist has experience dealing with OCD and teaching CBT with ERP – the recognized treatment for the disorder.

The back seat is not where you want to be. You want to be in the driver's seat where you can be in charge of getting better.

How to approach a GP

Talking about your OCD to your doctor can be a scary proposition. Many people find it incredibly difficult to talk about the scary thoughts they have or the compulsions they feel they have to perform over and over again. It can be extra challenging to talk about obsessions that have to do with your sexual orientation or children and sex.

Visiting your GP to start the process toward recovery is just the first step. Your GP doesn't need to know everything about your OCD since he/she will be recommending you to some kind of mental health service or therapist. Though many GPs have some experience dealing with OCD issues, not every GP has experience with every possible type of obsession and compulsion.

You can start by simply saying, "I think I have OCD," or "I think my child has OCD."

You can go a little further by explaining the theme of obsessions you or your child has, without going into specifics about the type of obsessions experienced. You can also talk broadly about the types of compulsions present.

The idea is to give your doctor enough information so he/she will know what to do – namely get you an appointment with someone who can help you.

What you should do if you know someone with OCD

Don't judge. Your child, friend, relative or spouse cannot control the intrusive thoughts they get. And they can't just stop their compulsions. They can learn to stop them, over time, with the right kind of therapy.

Get informed. The simple fact that you read this book puts you miles ahead with knowledge than the average person on the street when it comes to OCD. With a basic knowledge of the disorder, you can talk to the sufferer, understanding what is being said and offering constructive words in return.

Encourage. Be there. It can be incredibly difficult for the sufferer to give up his/her compulsions. Encouragement works and just being there to be a sounding board when things get frustrating can be very beneficial.

Don't engage compulsions. Many people with OCD get others around them ensnarled in their compulsions. They may demand that things be done a certain way or that some things not be touched. Doing compulsions for a sufferer is not helping them. It's just keeping the sufferer stuck. People want to help so the sufferer feels better but helping with compulsions only makes a bad situation worse. In a proper program of recovery involving a mental health professional, conversations will take place with the sufferer and you about slowing down and eventually stopping helping with compulsions. Make sure to have that conversation with the sufferer. Understand that you are doing a world of good by backing off from doing compulsions for the sufferer; hopefully the sufferer is well enough informed that he/she understands that it is for the best.

OCD resources

OCD Life
http://www.ocdlife.ca

International Obsessive Compulsive Disorder Found.
http://www.iocdf.org

OCD UK
http://www.ocduk.org

OCD UK Forums
http://www.ocdforums.org

OCD Stories
http://www.theocdstories.com

About the author

Dave Preston is an author, freelance writer and small town journalist. *The Little Book Of OCD* is his second book. He lives in British Columbia's Okanagan Valley with his wife Jackie, his son and the indelible memory of Miss Kitty.

You can help

If you enjoyed this book, if it changed your mind about what OCD is, if it made you think deeply, won't you consider logging onto your favorite online book retailer and leaving a review? It both helps the author and helps other readers discover this book.

Connect Online

www.OCDLife.ca
www.twitter.com/ocdlife

Truth be Told

A journey from the dark side of OCD

Dave Preston

Buy the incredible OCD memoir now!

After suffering in silence from horrible intrusive thoughts for nearly 40 years, Dave finds himself in the middle of a police investigation. Dave's world crashes around him and, in desperation, he seeks mental health help. He is diagnosed with an extreme mental disorder that not only answers why he had the terrible thoughts for so many years but also why the police showed up at his door.

As Dave takes steps to regain control over his life, he is faced with criminal charges of a despicable nature that leads to a court case with a surprise ending.

Truth be Told is the story of the dark side of OCD: living with it and recovering from it. It is a powerful, moving and inspiring story sure to make readers re-evaluate what they thought they knew about the disorder.

Read an excerpt from Truth be Told: A journey from the dark side of OCD...

Today mom went to the store by herself.

Sometimes we go together. It's not queer for a boy my age to go to the grocery store with his mom. Sometimes I get a treat and that's cool. Sometimes I go by myself. I can carry a paper grocery bag in one arm and steer my bike with the other hand, so I'm good to go.

"David, I'm going to the store." That's what she said before she walked out the door.

It would have been silly for me to tell her that the second the door clicked shut a timer began running in my head. I never told her about the timer and I didn't tell her today.

Tick, tock, goes the timer.

I know how far the grocery store is from our house. Five blocks. I know almost exactly how long it takes to drive there. It's a small store, so it doesn't take long to walk down every aisle and pick up the few things needed.

We never have a lot in the cupboards or fridge and mom only ever buys one or two bags of groceries at a time. There's time needed to go through the checkout, then it's out to the car and then the short drive home. I know how long it should take to buy groceries. The timer is meant to time how long it actually takes.

The house is quiet, save for the hum of the refrigerator and the sounds of a TV show.

Tick, tock.

I sit at the dining room table. I leaf through a hard cover book on astronomy. I like science and the book is one of many that mom and dad bought in a collection offered for sale on a TV commercial.

Tick, tock.

I flip the pages, look at the full colour pictures and read the captions underneath. The timer continues to run.

Tick, tock.

It must be getting close to time for her to come back. It's been the right amount of time.

I step away from the table and go to the kitchen window. Outside a car slowly plies the gravel street in front of our house, kicking up soft puffs of dust. The driveway is empty.

Where is she? It's been the right amount of time and she should be home by now. Shouldn't she? How long has it been? I think it's been long enough. She should be home.

It starts in my belly, uneasiness I have not become accustomed to, even though I've felt it many times before. The stirring becomes queasiness as I crane my neck to peer as far down the road toward the direction of the grocery store as I can, looking for mom's car.

Tick, tock.

Really, it has to be time. She should be done by now. She should be pulling up any second. What's taking so long? Where is she? She probably stopped to talk to someone or maybe the store is busy today. Why today? It's Tuesday. It's never busy on Tuesday. Where is she? What could she be doing?

I walk from the kitchen window back to the book on the table and flip a few pages. I walk back to the kitchen window. As I peer outside, my right hand forms a fist and begins squeezing and releasing, squeezing and releasing. It is spring and cool outside and my breath leaves a haze on the window as I breathe heavily against the pane.

Something happened to her. I know something happened to her. She tripped walking to her car with a paper bag of groceries, her feet went out from under her and her legs landed on the paved parking lot, and a car ran over them. Oh shit. Oh God. Oh God, did that happen? It's so real. There it is, the car driving slow, the black rubber tires slowly rolling up and over mom's legs, the scream, the look of horror on mom's face, the sound of cracking bone. Is that what happened?

Both my hands pump in unison as the window becomes too fogged to look out. I walk fast through the dining room to the living room and flip open the big, heavy curtain to get a better view through the picture window. My breathing comes in gasps, my eyebrows scrunch down and I start to scratch one arm, hard.

Tick, tock.

She got into an accident. She was driving home and a car came around the corner and smashed into her. I see it. I see the car in slow motion driving through the intersection and there's mom's car driving perpendicular to the other car and there's mom sitting behind the wheel and she doesn't see the other car and there it is, the big crash, the front end of the other car slowly pushing into mom's door and there's mom flopping around like a rag doll. She's crumpled over in the front seat and there's blood and she's not moving. Is that an ambulance siren I hear?

I pace from the living room to the kitchen, peer out the window then run back to the living room, throwing the curtain open. With my hands and face pressed against the glass, I can see clear down to the curve in the road but there's no car, no mom. I'm no longer thinking in my head. I'm screaming.

Where is she? She should be here by now! Something is wrong! Something is wrong with my mom! Where is she? Could she have slipped on the parking lot and been run over? Did she have an accident? She hit a gravel truck. That's what it is. She hit a gravel truck and, oh no, I'm going to lose my mom. For sure, something happened. It's way past time. She should be home by now.

Tears well up in my eyes. My face feels like it's so hot it's on fire. My fists pump rhythmically as I stare out the picture window and fog the glass with my hot breath. Another car, this one faster, drives along the road, blotting out the view toward the grocery store with a cloud of dust. I'm going to throw up. I feel every part of my body, as if little pinpricks are touching every part of skin from my toes to my head.

Tick, tock.

I'm alone. I'm so alone. Where is she?

Suddenly out of the mist of street gravel dust, a red form emerges. It's red, it's a car, and it's... mom. My eyes roll up into my head and I let out a sigh as I mouth the words, "Oh thank God."

The red Ford Maverick pulls into our driveway and I see mom behind the wheel. Everything is okay. Everything except the gut-wrenching feeling I have throughout my whole body. I know it will take hours for the feeling to go away.

Read more by purchasing Truth be Told: A journey from the dark side of OCD at your favorite online retailer! Buy it today!